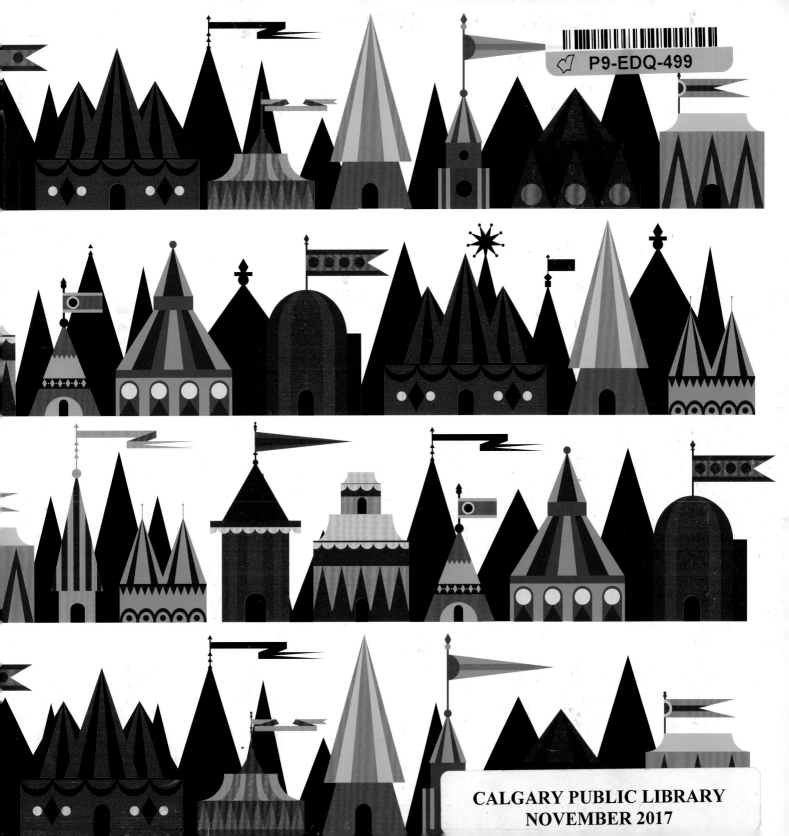

ABC

IS FOR

CIRCUS

by Patrick Hruby

AMMO

this book is dedicated to my sisters
Emily, Elizabeth, and Jennifer,
and to my wonderful nephew Zachary

 **IS FOR ACROBATS**

B IS FOR BIG TOP

C IS FOR CALLIOPE

D IS FOR DAREDEVIL

E IS FOR ELEPHANT

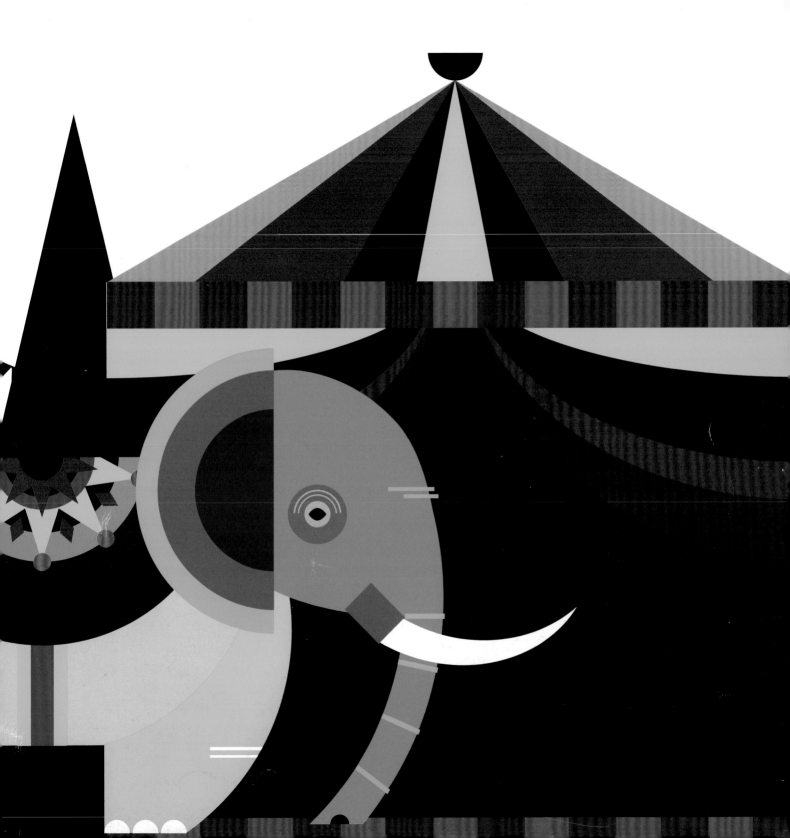

F IS FOR FIREWORKS

G IS FOR GIRAFFES

 **IS FOR HORSES**

IS FOR ICE CREAM

IS FOR JUGGLERS

K IS FOR KERCHIEF

L IS FOR LIONS

M IS FOR MONKEY

N
IS FOR NIGHTTIME

O IS FOR

P IS FOR PARADE

Q IS FOR QUEEN

R IS FOR RINGMASTER

S IS FOR SNAKE CHARMER

 IS FOR TIGER

Ü IS FOR UNICYCLE

V IS FOR VENTRILOQUIST

W IS FOR WEIGHTS

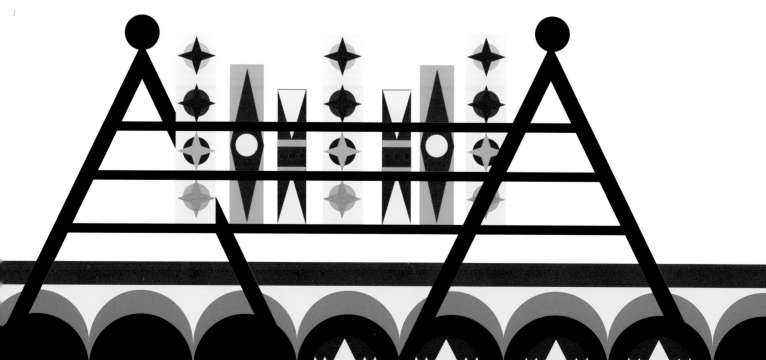

IS FOR X-RAY

Y IS FOR YELLOW

Z IS FOR ZEBRAS

© 2010 AMMO Books, LLC | All rights reserved
Printed in China
ISBN: 978-162326006-4

Art Direction: Gloria Fowler

For more children's books and products visit us at:
www.ammobooks.com

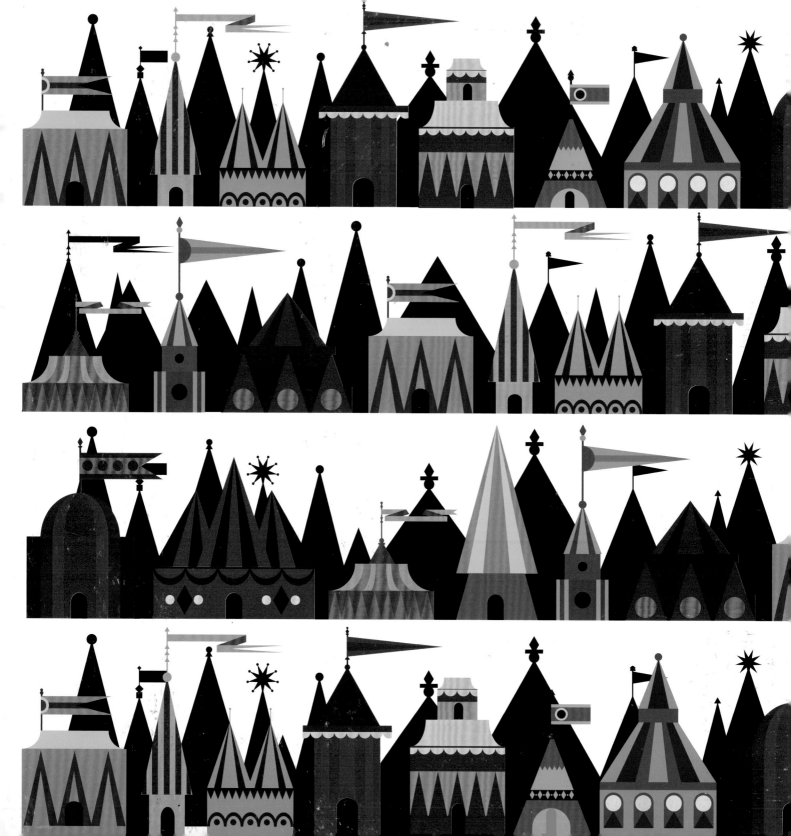